Cooking for the Criminally Insane

MADAME la Comtesse le Visage du Bouvier

Cooking for the Criminally Insane

madamelabouvier@gmail.com

facebook.com/madamelacomtesse

twitter.com/madamelabouvier

Copyright © Diane Stead 2014

ISBN 978-0-9939525-0-0

To all my husbands, past, present and future...

Table of Contents

Preface   *i*

COOKING FOR THE CRIMINALLY INSANE

Introduction	1
The Guest List	4
Ambience	7
The Importance of Wine	19
The Recipes	23
The Starters	26
Vegetable Soup	28
The Veggie Dish	29
Asparagus in White Sauce with Pancakes	30
The Fish Dish	31
Stuffed Squid	33
Dessert Already	34
Champagne Ice	36
The Meat Dish	38
Bunny in Beer	39
The Salad	41
Salad	43
The Sweet	45
Trifle, sort of	46
The Afters	47
Fruit and Cheese	49
And Finally...	51

PREPARING THE RECIPES

Vegetable Soup   54
French Pancakes with Asparagus in White Sauce   59
Stuffed Squid   63
Champagne Ice   67
Bunny in Beer   70
Salad   73
Trifle with Jack   77

Acknowledgements   *81*
Bibliography   *83*
A Note From the Publisher   *86*
The Reviews   *87*
About the Author   *88*

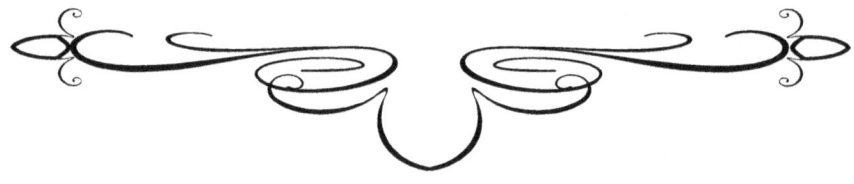

Preface

This volume was originally entitled, "Feast for the Criminally Insane" but alas, it seemed a little too pretentious, even for me. Nonetheless, the contents within are indeed the makings of a feast, a celebration.

I didn't always cook and I've certainly endured more unpalatable meals than you could shake a ladle at. You know those "little-out-of-the-way"-type restaurants that everybody raves about and it is a must-see and be-seen kind of destination. Where you sit in the almost complete darkness, which might be a blessing when you consider the rather rarified scent of the place. Then Raoul, your waiter arrives, unshaven with questionable fingernails that you choose to ignore but you can't help thinking you've seen him somewhere, a performer perhaps, Pricilla, Queen of the Desert, comes to mind, then you remember, you saw him at Il Convento at last summer's revue. He was the third drag queen on the left and he still hasn't taken off all his makeup. And with that same attitude he takes your order and just to be on the safe side you go with the chicken and are finally settling in with a glass of wine, when you hear the cat scream!

Oh yes, I have been to those places where you'll brave the food but you will absolutely not use their bathroom.

But such epicurean nightmares combined with plain old circumstance are what made me pick up the gauntlet and learn. Okay, more circumstance than nightmare but picture this.

It's a perfect Saturday afternoon at home on the estate, left to me by my second husband, the Count. Who, tragically was killed while on safari in Africa. He was hit by a tour bus. (Poor darling, probably tripped on his walker.) It must have been awful. There he was crossing the road to a bar somewhere in Kenya, when out of

nowhere WHACK! A whole bus load of Japanese. And don't those people like to take pictures. There was the Count, allover the road and within minutes, allover the internet. And me a widow, yet again, but I digress.

So here we are, me and Yves, the squeeze du jour, just reading newspapers, drinking tea, playing footsy, that sort of thing. When suddenly a raucous horde of fox-hunting, semi-inebriated, equestrian miss-fits converge on my door and

I've just fired the cook! *Quelle horreur.*

Order in, you say. Unfortunately, I am too far out of town for courteous delivery within thirty minutes.

What to do?

Happily, Yves knew how to make scrambled eggs and indeed, where to find the fry pan. (I probably should have married him). And I was more than adept at making Bloody Mary's with enough stuff in them (i.e. celery, hot sauce, horse radish), to almost double as a salad.

So, after dozens of eggs had hit the pan and several bottles of vodka had hit the dust, everyone eventually left with more than a pleasant glow. I guess it's good those horses knew their way home. Anyway, I had served my first meal! I was *chuffed*. Oh yes, did I mention we also had toast....

Cooking for the Criminally Insane

Introduction

I know how you feel. You find yourself somewhat gastronomically challenged. You've paid off the BMW, Range Rover's are starting to look good to you. You're maturing.

You've hired your cleaning lady full time even though you don't really need her and she still doesn't do windows, but she manages to make a day of plumping pillows and wiping dust off your almost-real Louis Quatorze furniture and the Baby Grand that you've never learned to play. You pay her handsomely because afterall she's been with you from the time you got your first job

and shared a roach ridden flat above a Chinese take-out with an enormous drag queen named CoCo who would never pick up a thing, except of course, men.

You've even hired someone to walk the dog. Not just any dog, mind you, but your Portuguese Water Dog, (that anyone else would call a poodle). You've reached a plateau in your life when you're convinced that after a hard day at the office, hiring and firing; a quick but grueling squash match with your boss, whom you know you could beat but it might cost you your job; and a few overpriced cocktails with  a sexy but disinterested certain party whose life revolves around social work, raising money for sick children, hiking, mountain climbing and herb gardening, but happens to have the body of your wildest fantasies.

After just such a day, you realize that you should be able to go home and cook something. Anything. Well, don't dismay, this book is for you.

Cooking is not only a joy (well, an acquired joy), it is almost a necessity. I mean, you can't dine out in fine restaurants every night. Well, ok, you could, but constantly eating delectable meals of exotic cuisine and being enveloped by the subtle aromas of inspired seasonings, not to mention the warming ambience of a perfect room and listening and enjoying the constant murmur of intelligent dinner conversation. You don't want this! You want to dine with your friends. And what better way to show them how much they mean to you then to prepare them a fine meal. If nothing else, it will give them something to talk about. And you know how they love to talk.

We will suffer through every painful step together. We'll sauté, braise, debone and even pronounce the name of every exciting dish (no matter what language it's in). Until that fateful moment arrives and you step out of your own miserable kitchen with a dinner fit for a queen and all of his friends. This will be your moment of grace, your finest hour. (Well, several hours actually when you include all the prep.) Your friends will be truly amazed. And as soon as they turn off the T.V. and wash their hands, they'll be allowed to taste it.

Who was it that said, 'the way to a man's heart is through his stomach'? (probably a surgeon). But that surgeon was right. Forget low-cal, low-fat, double decaf, steamed fish, skinned chicken, simulations of Styrofoam cartons. These recipes are gloriously made with REAL food! We're going to partake like the Europeans and eat anything!

So, buckle your belt. It may be the last time you can.

The Guest List

Choosing the right guests to intermingle and enjoy your feast is as important as the meal itself. You don't want people whose families have had an ongoing feud for centuries ever since the ancestor of one had the ancestor of another disemboweled and burned at the stake, then stole all their land. You don't want vegetarians. You don't want the woman who still wears a size four (I don't care if she is your best friend) she'll only pretend to eat and then rush off to the bathroom. You don't want anyone who is seriously on a diet, I mean, what's the point. And you definitely don't want any recovering alcoholics.

You want people with a bit of flesh on their bones. Jolly, congenial, intelligent people that can enjoy a clever anecdote without snorting their claret through their nostrils.

Never sit husbands and wives together. Sit them beside someone else's beleaguered spouse. If you had just spent hours getting all dressed up for a dinner party, choosing the right ensemble - a touch of Vivienne Westwood perhaps or Lagerfeld, (I know he's old, but he's still got it) but make sure it's absolutely nothing vintage or Madonna, come to think of it, that's pretty much the same thing -

would you want to rub elbows with the same person you just saw walking around the bathroom at home, flossing teeth and cutting toenails? I think not.

I tend to put my friends into colour categories, red or beige. (The truth be known, most of my friends are the scarlet type.) Don't sit them all together. Why should they have all the fun? It is best to "pepper" ones table with a beige person seated between two red ones and so on. It has been my experience that a beige person can indeed blossom into a red one after several courses, or drinks, or both.

For instance, I have a friend, the conductor of a major orchestra who starts off so beige, he won't talk to anyone about anything other than counterpoint. (I don't know what it is either.) But by mid-meal, and after several Long Island Ice Teas, various wines and a few beer chasers, he becomes downright animated.

Once, I thought we were going to have to get the police to convince him to put his clothes back on before we could pour him into a cab… but that's another story.

Equal numbers of the sexes is also not a requirement.

Some of my most colourful friends have a difficult time being put into either category safely.

Preferably invite people you like. People you don't like will eventually annoy you or worse, try and make you like them. You don't have time for this when you are serving the feast. Also, relatives can be tricky. They know your real age.

Only invite your boss if you are sure the other guests will behave. And this is always risky. Someone with loose lips is liable to remember the story that you regaled them with last Christmas, when you told everyone you know, about catching your boss with his/her pants down at the company party.

Don't invite your hairdresser unless you have absolutely no scars that he/she might have misconstrued as the result of expensive cosmetic surgery.

Don't invite anybody you owe and avoid the clergy.

Finally, the unspoken epitome of a successful dinner party rules – never book it for the day of the Super Bowl and absolutely NO children.

Ambience

Ambience can be many things. It can be the witty **bon mots** your guests fall all over each other to deliver. It can be the delicate aura of a fragrant candle. It can be those little finger towels in the bathroom that cost you a fortune (and your best friend just used one to take off her lipstick). It can be your place settings...

Ambience begins with you.

Madame de Place Pigalle, one of Paris's more celebrated courtesans, (although they're not really called that these days) has often said "you can't have enough flowers." Unfortunately when it comes to a dinner party and your dinner table, that is not true.

Flowers are beautiful, granted. But inevitably one or more of your guests will bring you an unwanted bouquet. (Perhaps some tick-in-

fested variety from their own garden that smells remarkably like Rover's 'eau de toilet' which this guest thinks speaks volumes of how close they perceive your personal relationship to be and you know they wouldn't have been invited if it wasn't for your box-boy at the supermarket canceling at the last minute.) Bear with it. These bouquets always show up just when something is boiling over on the stove, other guests are arriving at the rate of a tour bus unloading at a souvenir stand in Niagara Falls, and your phone is ringing off the hook with the first of the diners reporting in, that they have been delayed because they have to replace their temperamental teenage baby-sitter who has been grounded for wearing too much make-up. You graciously take a moment to smell the roses (not to mention clip them, find the proper vase to put them in, fill it with water AND search out an appropriate place of display!) then return to your duties as host/hostess only to find the guests you *really* wanted to impress have already poured their own drinks and stand clustered in your garden exchanging the most exquisite little stories that make no sense to you (but you laugh anyway) since you have barely caught the punchline.

Nevermind.

By now everyone has their first drink, or second (or, come to think of it, who knows how much they've had before they arrived?) and you are taking on the attitude of the congenial, relaxed host/hostess. (Well, as relaxed as one can be after cooking all day and drinking sherry and not really being sure if you remembered to feed the dogs or put on deodorant!)

The music you have chosen will make all the difference.

Now, I know we all love Bruce Springsteen, BUT, some tunes are just not dinner party fare. Frankly playing anything "pop" can be dangerous. It can pigeonhole you, or worse, give away your age! Jazz... well everybody says they like it until they have to hear it for more than an hour... folk, country, blues – dinner party suicide, somebody is liable to sing along. I suggest good ol' classical. It's unobtrusive. It's delicate but not annoying (generally) and it has a certain elegance. Let's face it, you want your guests to be impressed not only with the meal but with your inherent good taste all round. Just be sure to avoid Wagner and keep the overall decibels down because it has been my experience that classical music can creep up on you. (There you are, in a quiet conversation with some handsome thing, almost at each others elbows while in the background the piccolos pick. Then suddenly the orchestra goes for it. Fortissimo, I think they call it. The person you were in conversation with has flipped his claret over his shoulder and you've jumped so high that the gorgeous new fall/hairpiece that no body knew you were wearing, hits the roof and takes it's own sweet time returning to your head.)

So to re-cap. Let's assume you have just the right bouquets strategically appointed throughout the house, i.e. on top of the piano, on the mantle beside the Italian silver picture frame displaying a gentleman in a second world war uniform that you tell everyone is your granddad (when in fact it's your father). There are smaller arrangements in the bathrooms and don't ever forget setting up your personal bog because even if you have fifteen baths in the house, one guest will always find their way into your own private domain.

Finger towels are a must; cute little individual soap pieces shaped like something interesting… i.e. sea-shells, mini jewel boxes, Jaguar keys; fragrances – mens and womens and definitely none with the word 'Tester' on them from your friend at Estee Lauder; ladies personal hygiene products discreetly wrapped in non-commital paper (I know a woman who always makes a big deal of asking for them in front of the company, even though she hasn't had any use for them since at least the last millennium. Really My Dears, it's a case of *…and a star shall rise in the East…* if you get my drift); and several casual displays of photographs of you laughing with one lover or another at some fabulous vacation spot. If you have won any awards i.e. Emmy, Tony, Pulitzer prize..

display them in a 'couldn't care less' sort of place like the top of your fridge or toilet.

Now, let's set the table.

In order to accommodate ten full place settings for the feast for the Criminally Insane, it should already be evident that you will require a table roughly the size of a little league baseball diamond. Since we are basing this on the premise that there are no servants, it would be ideal to have large sidetable conveniently situated near the host/hostess. (Borrow one if you have to, furniture does not have to match unless of course it's modern.)

Your table will have a low-lying floral centre-piece and candles to begin with. The centre-piece does not have to be flowers every time, a tasteful sculpture will work as well, as long as it's not a bust of Elvis or a sensual mold depicting naked bodies of two people intertwined. (This can really set the conversation back or forward, depending on how you look at it). Napkins (linen only, but you knew that) should be obviously displayed so no one forgets to use theirs. The fan-shape thing has been done to death, I still prefer a simple clutched piece of fabric rolled in a wide band of ivory…, silver…., brass. (Forget those hippy wood-carved rings that you bought in Arizona in the sixties. Uncool.)

Name tags are a must. There is nothing more disconcerting than having to run for the phone or answer the door just as your guests approach the table and everyone stands around like so many frightened starlings, waiting for you to seat them. Also, this allows you to choose who you want sitting next to you. (Why not? It's your party and you've done all the work, why should you be stuck with your accountant?) It also gives you a little leverage with

the intrigues of your company. Be creative. It might be amusing to seat that handsome single guy that you know is a boob-man right next to your old flame's new wife who just happens to have enough décolleté to choke a horse.

China and cutlery should be removed after each course, except if you are going Greek, at which time you just keep stacking it until finally your guests can no longer see each other across the table. This is a tradition to show how wonderful the repast has been. At one meal at the **Daughters of Helen** I kept talking and drinking long after dessert and when I got up to leave, it turned out, me and one old guy, who was now sound asleep, were the only ones left. I had been babbling out some of my best stories to myself for an hour and a half. It's true.

Anyway, if someone has used the wrong implement, and they will, ignore it. Too bad if later they have to use the butter knife to eat their crème caramel. Put it all out. If you're serving fish, dig out those fake-ivory handled, etched silver atrocities that someone gave you at your first wedding and are still wrapped in the cellophane. Matching china is nice if you're the royal family but mixing and matching patterns can appear eclectic even if brought on by necessity. For instance, if you're going with the silver-edged Wedgewood but don't have enough soup bowls than hopefully the Dollar store specials will not look too out of place. Also, serving on different complete place settings is ***tres elegant***. A different one for each guest can be wonderful as long as you don't have to resort to your mother's souvenir plates of the Queen's coronation or anything from Disney.

Stacking an entire place setting can also have its drawbacks. As wonderfully pretentious as it might seem, imagine if one of your guests is, shall we say, diminutive. So much so that he/she can't see over this fantastic display of expensive dishes and has to carry on a conversation with nothing showing but their eyebrows. Even worse, you're liable to be asked to bring in a phonebook for this person to sit on. Just not done.

You can never find the phonebook when you need it anyway.

The finesse with which you serve a meal is an intricate part of the ambience. Serve the soup sitting down, be "mum", as each guest hands around the soup bowls and you dispense from that spectacular tureen you snapped up at a garage sale. Your guests are still relatively sober and this creates the warm feeling of camaraderie and well-being. Hovering over the guests to ladle it out tends to reduce the ambience to that of the paranoia of a Sally-Ann soup kitchen.

Inevitably there will be one course that will keep you in the kitchen for an extended time. It's alright really, it gives your guests a chance to get to know each other, so clearly you're not going to miss much. Or, if your house is outfitted for an intercom system, just turn it on. This and some creative electronics taped discreetly under the table will ensure that you don't miss anything anyone is saying about you. For that matter, if you're any good at Audio/Visual in the first place, why not install mini-cameras. It's amazing what can go on under the table during a dinner party. Footsies, is just the least of it!

If any of the guests graciously offer to help pick up and remove some of the plates take a moment to consider their state of sobriety. You don't want broken Royal Doulton allover the oriental rugs. But sometimes this can turn out to be a blessing. It works as a sort of guilt snowball so that after each course a new guest will offer their services so as not to be outdone. With any luck, they might even offer to do the dishes.

Always present the main course with as much fanfare as possible. Bagpipes and Mariachis however effective, have been done to death. Those Chippendale dancer guys may be great eye-candy, but they can take away your thunder. This is about YOU, your statement. Make it count. Personalize it a little.

I have a friend Giselle (Gizzy for short) that went through a "Cirque de Soliel" period. It started out with her obsession for Las Vegas. She would fly down every few weeks and sit in on one of the Cirque shows. (It was either that or Celine Dion, so I ask you, was there a choice?) Anyway, she studied the magicians with a passion and actually got pretty good at some of their tricks. At one of her soirees she presented her main course in a puff of smoke. Unfortunately one of the guests panicked and through expensive Beaujolais all over her beef bourguignon. We ate it anyway.

But the best story of her Cirque days was when she actually trained with one of the acrobats. (I told you she was obsessed.) You must have seen on TV the girl performer who wraps herself in a drape, storeys high in the air and gently lowers herself to the floor by unwrapping. Gizzy learned to do that! Seriously. Anyway, she practiced and practiced until she pretty much had it down and one day, she wanted to surprise her boyfriend when he arrived at her condo. The trouble is he never did arrive. That is to say, he called her answering machine and told her he wouldn't be seeing her anymore (apparently his wife was getting wind of it), so there was Gizzy dangling from the 12 foot ceiling listening to this guy dumping her, with nothing on but a curtain when she realized she had tied the wrong knot or something and she couldn't get it loose. She yelled and screamed a bit but you know how soundproof those expensive buildings are. Anyway, she tried to swing herself over by the window to get anybody's attention but to what end. She's on the 44th floor.

Well finally, two days later, her cleaning lady let herself in. Now just imagine the mess! Not to mention the fright. Anyway, Gizzy was unconscious, stark naked and dangling from the ceiling. She did survive, of course, but unfortunately, her relationship with the cleaning lady that had worked for her for 20 years, didn't. That poor woman bolted the minute Gizzy had hit the ground and hasn't been seen or heard from since. Gizzy said, after the cleaning lady had cut the cord and Gizzy fell to the floor, the cleaning lady kept praying out loud and blessing herself as she made a beeline for the elevator. I kid you not.

So maybe nothing quite so acrobatic. But perhaps a little magic, a puff of smoke, a flash of light. You'll think of something.

Finally, be prepared for anything. The attitude of the host/hostess is as much a part of the ambience as the meal itself. There may be upsets.

For instance, your best friend, now slurring a lot, laughing way too loud and tipping ever so slightly in her ten-inch heels, graciously attempts to help clear the table. You try to stop her but she grabs a whole load of your best wine glasses and staggers off towards the kitchen. That is of course, just when the dog comes shooting into the room, after the cat, with complete disregard for your dinner party and runs straight between your friend's legs (because, as usual, her damn skirt is too short) and sends her flying into the sideboard.

Or worse yet. An affable gent has

surreptitiously loosened his belt and trousers under the table while overeating and before standing up to go to the loo, he re-fastens everything and includes a piece of the tablecloth into his zip. He stands smartly to attention and takes half of the remaining dishes with him.

Show no tears. "Life is a Cabaret" you keep telling yourself, and leave your misery for after your guests leave, probably sometime near dawn having drained the last vestige of alcohol in your possession and having decimated several of your antique crystal glasses that can never be replaced.

You are now alone and left to face the kitchen! "And I love a Cabaret….."

Bon Chance!

The Importance of Wine

Very.

Who has ever heard of a dinner party, a feast, without wine? (Dinner without wine is called supper and it's served in Florida at 4 in the afternoon). This is not that.

Wine is everything. It can be soothing. It can be jolly. It can be uninhibiting. It can be crisp and clear, bubbly and pink or deep red and mysterious. It is as old as time. It should never have a screw-top or a funny name.

Some of your friends may delight in saying that they don't really drink. In my experience, these people drink anything and lots of it. Be prepared. A well-stocked bar is a thing of beauty.

To start, a dry sherry can be wonderful. You get to use those lovely delicate little glasses with the floral etchings that your Grandmother left you. The glasses are often bell-shaped and elegant but you can't put more than a thimble-full in them at one time, so keep the bottle handy.

Sherry is meant to be from Spain. It can be from South Africa if you don't mind it a little sweeter and with a punch that could level Mike Tyson. It should be sipped and never forget how easily it can go down.

White wine, le Vin Blanc, is a staple. It should be crisp and pale and travel well from a famous chateau or ancient vineyard. Then again, it can be ordinaire and have no redeeming qualities and be the plonk you bought at your local supermarket. Don't worry. Chill it to almost freezing and no one will know the difference. Ice cubes are not an option so make sure it never reaches room temperature.

Decanting white wine is complete folly unless of course, you have bought the grocery store variety and the label on the bottle is a child-like drawing of a cat or a bull. Then by all means, decant. This is assuming you have a few of those fake crystal "treasures" that you received at one wedding or another from your semi-illiterate cousins with as much sophistication as Tammy Fay Baker, (don't be shocked, we all have those in the family) and no matter how many garage sales you have stuck them out on the table for purchase (or free) absolutely not one soul even looked at them. Who knew they'd come in handy?

White wine is considered the proper potable for fish dishes. I've never been that regimented when serving dinner. Being a die-hard red wine drinker, I could sip it with kippers at breakfast. Or even without the kippers.

Red wine, le Vin Rouge, is a much more important purchase but you need not take out a second mortgage to buy a good one.

I've always considered myself a connoisseur of cheap wine. Forget trendy, ostentatious wines-du-jour or the favorite vintage of your dentist who runs six miles a day to keep in shape and who thinks bicycling should be as rigorous as the 'Tour de France' and probably only drinks red wine by the glass. There are a few simple rules to buying le Vin Rouge. First, whichever county it does comes from, the vineyards should be old, the sun hot (and I don't mean just for two months of the year) and generally the indigenous people would rather sit with their entire families around café tables on a sultry afternoon discussing politics than lining up at a gargantuan theme park for a ride on the "Mass Mountain Stomach Disposal Unit". Usually the people of the countries with good wine don't even know what a theme park is AND get this, they don't care!

Should it happen that one of your guests brings a better bottle of wine than the one you're serving, no problem. This is when the decanting principal kicks

in. Decant your household plonk and before anyone gets to taste it, do the old lifting the glass to the light, swishing it around in your mouth and looking at it pensively for a moment, routine. It assures everyone that this must indeed be a superior vintage and how lucky they all are to have been invited to this meal with such an authority entertaining them. Then stash the better wine for another day.

Les Recettes
~ or ~
The Recipes

Much consideration and expertise has gone into the organization and planning of the "Feast for the Criminally Insane". A fine meal is orchestrated, and as you prepare this repast, consider yourself nothing less than the maestro. We'll imagine for now, that you have no servants to cook, no servants to serve, no servants to clean up, and well, just no servants. (Makes you wonder why you're bothering.) Granted, although this is not something you can put on a resume, the experience of preparing from scratch, dealing with the wrong meats from the butcher, the threats from the butcher's wife (because he stayed too long on that particular delivery), having to serve non-gluten bread (which is as chewable as a wet gym towel and without the same nutritional benefit), the experience of preparing and serving the feast will create enough fodder for your barroom conversation for months to come.

No detail will be overlooked.

Each of these exciting courses has been adapted from classic menus of grand dinners. A similar soup may have been enjoyed by Henry VIII himself, as a late night pick-me-up before gallantly dragging himself back into the royal boudoir to yet another young bride.

The vegetable crepes would surely have made the delicate mouth of the ill-fated Marie Antoinette water. Perhaps if she had been quoted as saying "let them eat crepes!" her head would have remained on her shoulders. Of course, this is only speculation.

And the Calmar! I have read that Alexander the Great trekked across half of the known world of his time, in search of the ultimate squid. Apparently, when nearing a fishing village on the Aegean, he caught a whiff of calamari on the grill being bathed in a funny little wine that only the Greeks understand – Retsina.

He jumped down from his elephant and rushed into a private home where a peasant woman of enormous girth and an unfortunate moustache was about to serve up. He fell to his knees and shouted "OPAA!", or so the story goes.

Let's not forget the plat principe. This particular dish was rumoured to be a favorite of the Mad King of Bavaria, Ludwig II. It is said, the troubled monarch had been known to visit the barns and henhouses of his glorious castles to talk to his dinner before it became his dinner. His closest aide (and a terrible traitor) had reported that the King had spent three full days in the barns with his favorite cow, Brunhilda, trying to convince her that her demise was for the good of the state (or steak, as the pundits of the day had it).

A royal feast indeed and all recipes included will be to serve ten people. A meal of this magnitude would be madness otherwise. Make sure you have bought all the needed ingredients prior to execution. There is nothing  more distracting than having to call your local supermarket on the day of the feast, in a complete panic, just to find out that they don't carry anchovies! ANY anchovies!

Your friends will be dazzled by your new-found culinary expertise. You'll walk proudly with a different gait (of course, some detractors might insist this is due to all the sherry you've consumed while cooking).

D'APPARAT POUR LES CRIMINEL A FOU will be the one meal you will prepare in your life that no one can forget! No matter how hard they try.

Le Premier Plat
— *or* —
The Starters

Many would call this the appetizer. I prefer not. Taco chips with salsa is an appetizer to some. And if you have invited your entire bowling team, why not? But then again, if you've invited a bowling team I doubt very much, that you will be reading this book in the first place.

The first course will set the mood. This is why soup has become a favorite. It is warming (unless you're serving it cold), it should enliven the appetite, so chowders are out. And it lets everyone get rid of at least the first piece of cutlery.

Your guests may still be sipping on their pre-dinner cocktail, which is fine. But a crisp, sparkling wine (or champagne, if you can afford it) will go down nicely. Rose is another alternative.

Never serve too much soup and certainly no tacky crackers.

I once had a friend who actually carried her own saltines! It was the wildest thing. Everywhere she went it sounded like she was dancing a shuffle on a 1940's dance floor. Anytime she would take a dollar out of her bag, which wasn't often, the money would be covered in crumbs. No one wanted to take it, which is how she saved up enough to buy that trailer in Florida. But I digress.

Soup warms the soul. And since it is the beginning of your wonderful meal, it is also a great way to warm up the early conversation, while everyone is still speaking to each other.

Le Potage des carotte, les pois, le mais, le Poivron vert, l'Oignon, le Poireau et les Champignon avec un Paprik

~ or ~

Vegetable Soup

Vegetable soup can be many things. It can be a robust stew of garden delights, so thick that a waxed turnip could go undetected. This is the rustic version favored by farmers, outdoorsmen and women who drive Harleys and call themselves 'Bernie'.

Veggie soup can be a fragile broth made from the essence of some long past-its-prime plant matter that should have been thrown out but instead was boiled beyond recognition and then served without any regard for human life. This is the institutional variety that is generally served in hospitals to people who have mostly given up on living anyway.

Vegetable soup can be red, it can be green, it can be black if enough beans are used. (But we certainly don't want to serve anything with beans this early in the feast!)

Vegetable soup is as old as Mother Nature but not nearly as unpredictable.

(All recipes at the back)

Le Deuxieme Plat
~ or ~
The Veggie Dish

The dinner is in the early stages. Your guests are still complimenting each other, whether they mean it or not. They're discussing financial portfolios and significant universities for their children and chic cabarets in the south of France. The women still have their lipstick on (and not on their teeth. Not yet.) and everyone is smiling. You could cut the camaraderie with a knife.

It's generally about this time, that your one late arrival, arrives. This is the guest that comes through the door with reckless abandon and stops the dinner party in its tracks. Conversations are severed in mid-sentence while everyone is forced to listen to the long drawn out excuse that nobody wants to hear. Especially you.

You dash to the kitchen and bring the late comer some soup while your next course is wilting. After a few discreet tears, you fix your mascara and bravely decide to push on. It's time to serve the veggie dish.

We're not going to serve just any vegetable either, oh no, we're going to serve asparagus. And you'll soon learn how special that can be when you try to buy it out of season.

Les Crepe Francaise avec la Crème blanche et les Asperges
— or —
Asparagus in White Sauce with Pancakes

There has long been an unreasonable fascination with asparagus. In parts of Europe an entire week is dedicated to eating it, talking about it, a veritable worship of it. The asparagus festival in the Netherlands is famous throughout the world and by all accounts a must-see. The Europeans prefer the white spears which are often more tender (not to mention, more expensive), but the green ones will do.

Asparagus was known to be a favorite of Cleopatra. She would personally choose the most perfect spears and then have them dipped in gold. Then they would be arranged on a chain that Cleo would wear around her neck. (You can see a later adaptation worn by Liz Taylor in the movie.)

Early geishas also saw the beauty of this vegetable and would dry out the spears to use as hair ornaments and the really fat ones as chopsticks. Asparagus was by far the most sought after vegetable for an art form, even more than the venerable artichoke. Imagine what Warhol could have done with it, if he hadn't been so preoccupied with soup cans.

Le Poisson
~ or ~
The Fish Dish

The fish dish can be so many things, from Maridas as the Greeks call panfried smelts to Poached Salmon to… well… our little adventure.

Even weekend vegetarians and/or people on diets will eat fish. (Grilled, no oil, no flavor.) It's considered brain food. North Americans generally just don't like looking at it, let alone cleaning it. If they eat fish at all it's usually some bland white fillet from the frozen food aisle that they later deep fry to taste like chicken and then smother in catsup. This lamentable display bears no resemblance to the meaty, delicious species of the deep available to us.

Natives of the Mediterranean coast like to eat ALL the fish including the heads. I've seen more arguments arise when one person beats another person to the head with the biggest eyes. I've tried the heads myself (after several liters of wine) and can honestly say they are delicious. Just make sure they are well grilled and not the size of Moby Dick.

The more bones a fish has, the more flavor. And filleting it at the table for your guests can be sheer entertainment. But forget that, we're serving squid.

By now your guests should be drinking wine. If someone is still on bourbon or Long Island iced tea, it's time to insist they move on, (that is with the hope that they can still move at all.)

Time to crack open the white wine. This should be a truly dry wine (a vintage that almost makes you pucker and sends a shiver down your spine upon first taste). If you're serving a vin ordinaire for the financially challenged with a bouquet like an old bucket of plaster, I suggest none of your guests smell the cork (or cap in this case) for fear of cutting their nose.

Les Calmar dans la Casserole des Tomate
~ or ~
Stuffed Squid

To begin with, let's just call it calamari. Everyone eats calamari these days but tell them that it's really just plain old squid and they'll berate you with a litany of tired clichés. i.e. "Squid! You've got to have more teeth than I've got to chew it!" or that old nugget – "Always tastes like rubber bands to me." First of all, if these are your guests, my sympathies, and secondly, don't tell them what it is until they've asked for more. This is when you can really have some fun with them.. i.e. "Yeah, You'd never know this was squid… except of course, for the little tentacles. They taste great for bottom feeders, don't you think? Slippery little devils, aren't they?"

If you lose any of your guests at this stage, don't worry, they'll be back. They can't spend the entire night in the bathroom.

Le Sorbet
~ or ~
Dessert Already?

There has been much speculation about the origins of sorbet. Volumes have been written on just this subject. The most colorful tale takes place in France. It has been said that a few centuries back, a rather large personage of the French royal house was always insisting on dessert several times through the course of any one meal. Legend has it, that when he had indeed grown too large for the royal wardrobe, a dietician from the nearby village was summoned and put to the onerous task of satisfying the regal sweet tooth while not overstuffing the now porcine features of the head of the royal house. No easy task.

She labored for days, enduring the wrath and abuse of the royal fatso, (which is of course, how we know the dietician to be a woman), constantly under the dark shadow of Madame de Guillotine. And after several close calls of ducking the barrage of inanimate platefuls of experimental dessert items that had not pleased his majesty, the tired little dietitian had been

stripped naked, covered with honey and turned out of the castle. (The idea being that the local wild animals would soon discover the pathetic creature and fall upon her and consume her.) But as it turned out, the animals were all snoring it off in their hibernation hideouts when an unexpected snow storm blew threw the area and the honey dripping off the woman got all mushed up with the snow. The poor little dietician had collapsed only yards from the castle and was about to perish in the cold, when the royal fatso had snuck out to go to the village and buy himself a couple of Snickers bars, or whatever they called them in those days. He tripped on her and went face down in the honey and ice. The rest is history.

Other experts would say that sorbet was solely intended to clean the palate, refresh it, and prepare it for the taste experience to follow.

Whatever. Remember one thing, sorbet is definitely not icecream and we never serve more than a scoop.

Le Sorbet du Champagne
~ or ~
Champagne Ice

You may have already been drinking champagne with the previous courses or all day for that matter. (Let's face it, any excuse.) But now we're going to eat it.

The beauty of this little respite to our glorious feast is that sorbet can be made from almost anything. Citrus fruit, berries, melons have all had their day in the sun, but I chose champagne because I have never met anyone who wasn't in possession of a bottle of some horrific sparkling wine with a pretentious label inferring champagne. You know the stuff I mean. Someone from the office gave it to you last Christmas after someone had given it to them the Christmas before. You'd give it away yourself except you can't remember the jerk that gave it to you in the first place because it had been cleverly disguised in a 'Season's Greetings' bottle bag worth more than the plonk itself and although you'd love to give it back to the same person, you can't remember who it was. It probably has a cute drawing of a duck or teddy bear on the label and just looking at it can start the aura of one of those terrible migraines you get when you

drink anything domestic.

What better way to get rid of this insidious potable than to eat it? Trust me, no one will really taste the full horror of the vintage because we're going to use sugar in the recipe and besides, your guest's palates will still be reeling from the previous course.

Le Plat Principe
~ or ~
The Meat Dish

Meat. Flesh of an animal. It's not really clear when or where man decided to eat animals. But if the placement of the eyes on a human (i.e. looking forward – the hunter) as opposed to the eyes of say, a deer (i.e. on the side of the head - the hunted), then it would seem that man has been a carnivore through a long period of evolution. That may be why you never hear of anyone eating their cat. And if you do, I suggest you report it.

I still giggle at that old sci-fi television show where the aliens are taking over the earth and everybody is panicking. Then finally the head alien presents to the masses of hysterical humans a book entitled "To Serve Man" and everyone applauds thinking well that's more like it. Until they realize "To Serve Man" is actually a cookbook!

Dinner just wouldn't be dinner without the principal dish. This is where fanfare and drama of presentation kick in. Make it big or go home, I say. This is the main course. This is the main event!

Le Lapin de Madame la Comtesse avec Biere Allemande
~ or ~
Bunny in Beer

Rabbit has long been a staple of humankind. Those dear little furry creatures with the twitching noses are not only cute, they're delicious. Don't feel guilty, they breed like… well, you know. I recommend buying your bunnies already prepared by the butcher. You don't want Peter Cottontail with a tiny bullet-hole in his head, sitting on your counter looking surreally like some child's Easter present.

The association of rabbit with beer probably became most prominent in the sixteenth century. It's thought that it may have been the only game the hordes of big bad mead-swilling hunters of the time could bag. Great hunting parties of unshorn men wrapped in curious non-combative, weekend-wear-style armor roamed the rolling hills outside of their castles, drinking from goat-skins and firing arrows at anything that moved. Occasionally, they hit a rabbit.

But even before that, further back through the mists of time, it is well documented how primeval man fed his family by roasting the carcass over a spit. Nothing, in those days, was ever wasted. Mr. Cro-Magnon was probably the first guy to present his bride

 with a fur coat and what do you think? Rabbit, of course. And when Mrs. Cro-Magnon had more fur coats than she had the closet space for, Mr. Cro-Magnon started using the rabbit's coat for footwear. Thus, those fluffy slippers with the long ears that we've all received from a maiden aunt at one birthday or another.

If your guests are the skittish types, don't mention the word rabbit. Call it Lapin (pronounced la – pa(n)). It doesn't sound so carnal when said in French. And not only that, your guests will think you've mastered a new language. Win-win.

Le Temps a manger votre Verts
~ or ~
The Salad

The salad course is often served before the main dish but that's more of a North American thing, like bar-b-ques and Kraft dinner. In the context of the feast, the salad is served with a definite purpose - to help digestion. Like the sorbet, it too can clean the palate.

By now your guests are all complaining about being stuffed. This is an excuse. Don't buy it. If your salad is as appealing as the previous dishes, they will eat it.

There is a particular school of thought that teaches that human beings were meant to eat ONLY greens. Herbivorous mammals, they call us. I don't completely disagree with this theory. After all, if we only ate veggies we would all be our perfect body weight, or less. Our skin would clear up. We would probably read Russian novels instead of watching T.V. We would actually enjoy jazz. And there would be no wars, because we wouldn't have the strength to lift a gun.

Salad is a lighter moment in our feast. Ideally, we present a humungous bowl resembling a 4th century artifact, brimming with delightfully tossed vegetables of various colors and textures that appear to have been casually thrown in. Little regard is given to the hour it took to wash, chop and tear these natural treasures not to mention the price out of season. Don't expect accolades for the salad course.

Fresh and crisp are our words du momente. Nothing is worse than a salad that looks like it's been sitting under an old Chevy during an oil change. Color is the other working definitive. If everything in the bowl is green, then you really lose your audience.

Inevitably there will be some boorish guest (probably your soon to be ex-boyfriend) who declines the salad and heads out of the room to check the football score. Ignore him. You can deal with him later. Threats work sometimes – no salad, no dessert. Or better still, if you don't mind seeing grown men cry, tell them there will be no liqueurs unless they eat their salad.

Les Legumes verte et la Laitue Americaine
~ or ~
Salad

I once lost a false eyelash in a salad. I assume it fell off when I was doing the tossing in front of everyone at the table. My friend, Gizzy, motioned something to me. She kept frantically batting her eyes and putting the back of her hand to her forehead. It was so Scarlett O'Hara that I didn't pay that much attention. (Gizzy is well known for her amateur theatrics). Anyway, as far as I know, the eyelash was never found.

It wasn't until later, around 3 a.m. when I was removing my usual ton – ton and a half of makeup that I realized something was amiss. Gad, I was a vision. No lipstick for probably the last 4 hours, my hair had taken on a life of its own and only one eye was actually still done up in full make-up. That eye looked like a prosthesis, like it was made of glass. It was the poster from Clockwork Orange. I looked like an aging punk-rock star.

Some of my guests had taken pictures throughout the evening and the only thing I could think about, was how was I going to keep those photos off of the internet!

Anyway, back to salad. Throw everything in. Fruit, nuts, all those veggies, but I would resist stick-on fingernails and false eyelashes or any jewelry that you might regret losing.

L'orgasme pour la Bouche
~ or ~
The Sweet

Some of your guests may have spent the entire meal anticipating dessert. Others may no longer be sitting upright. But whatever the status of your party, dessert is the subtle anti-climax we've all patiently been waiting for. It can leave you breathless after the grand fireworks of a Baked Alaska or Cherries Jubilee. It can be as divine as a Hazelnut Meringue that makes you feel certain you've had a religious experience. Chocolate Mousse can make the earth move for some. And after recovering from the thick sweet cream of an Éclair exploding in your mouth, you might find yourself reaching for a cigarette, even if you don't smoke.

But the D'APPARAT POUR LES CRIMINEL A FOU has already been a baronial meal of such proportion that a little restraint is called for. It's time for something simple and self-effacing – a Trifle.

L'enremets Rustique avec les Peche dans le Jaques Daniels
~ or ~
Trifle, sort of

Trifle is yet another opportunity to cook with alcohol. That sherry you have been enjoying earlier in the day will come in handy. Brandy is good. And believe it or not, even bourbon can add the elusive dimension of drama. The first thing to be sure of is that you have the pre-requisite large glass serving bowl. Trifle should be seen from all angles.

Trifle does not keep well so we're not going to make a huge one. Trifle is international. Similar puddings can be found allover the world. It is rich and creamy and easy to make and it is rumoured to have been a favorite or Queen Victoria herself. (And that lady liked to eat!)

To me, trifle has religious connotations. I've never attended a church function that didn't serve one variation or another. Sponge cake is the norm but we're going to use bread instead. Course country bread makes the dessert less sweet and seems to absorb the alcohol better. And if your guests eat enough alcohol there is still a chance that they won't decimate you liqueur stash later, n'est pas?

Apres la Fete...
~ or ~
The Afters

By now the conversation has turned to baseball teams, celebrity rehab and politics. Time to change that channel before they get into religion! Rumbling complaints about dead derrieres permeate the atmosphere. Still, no one has yet called a cab. Those that have been slumped down in their chairs for the better part of the last course, sit up, bright-eyed, rejuvenated. The pink has returned to their cheeks. They start telling jokes that bored you when you first heard them a few hours ago. A new camaraderie is evident. Your guests are smiling, giggling even, in anticipation. And what could be the cause of this late meal phenomena? The serving of the liqueurs of course! And not just any liqueurs. YOUR liqueurs!

Much has been written about these sweet, potent, let's not forget expensive, after-dinner treats. They are usually made from fruit and occasionally spices. They are often associated with religious orders. Probably because ever since the middle ages monks and cloistered nuns seem to be the principal purveyors. This could be due to the enormous orchards and ancient vineyards that have been kept for centuries by our more pious members of society. Or just the fact, that being locked up with all that perpetual chanting and celibacy made you wanna have a little drinkie.

There was even a rumour that the Inquisition was really nothing more than a fact finding mission by the Spanish to uncover the secrets of the liqueur-making craft. Joan of Arc, may have been burned at the stake, because she would not divulge the secret of Amaretto. George would not have had to face that dragon if only he'd fess up to how he made Grand Marnier. But this is medieval gossip.

Whatever the background, one truth prevails. Several of your closest friends drinking several mini-glasses of your best liqueurs will cost you a small fortune. Thank goodness for duty-free, is all I can say.

Le plat du Fruit de la Saison et le Fromage assortie
~ or ~
Fruit and Cheese

Many of my contemporaries would argue that the fruit and cheese comes before dessert. But as stated previously, with friends like mine, anxiously awaiting the liqueurs, it would be folly not to serve them something to nibble on. It could mean the difference between your friends walking out or passing out.

Buy your cheese from a cheese merchant. It's definitely one of those things that "you get what you pay for". A puny piece of supermarket cheddar that has just been unwrapped from its vacuum-sealed plastic, can put a true epicurean into culinary shock. Forget anything with a label reading "mild". You don't want something that could be mistaken for soap. I find a good rule of thumb is to choose cheese that children will not eat.

Three varieties is the norm. Consider a strong creamy blue cheese of sorts, i.e. Stilton, Roquefort or even Limburger if you've got the ventilation for it. A soft cheese i.e. Brie, Camembert, Edam. Include a chunky orange Cheddar to give the platter some

colour and give any relatives you may have invited, something to reach for that they recognize.

Grapes, pears, apples work fine. A good French or Italian baguette or English water biscuits cut the cheese, as it were. And finally, and above all, relax! Except for that war zone that is now your kitchen and will take 3 to 4 hours to clean-up, and the inevitable possibility that you may have to arrange sleeping quarters for a few of your guests that have quietly disappeared somewhere under the table, you are through for the night!

and Finally...

Many guests have left but inevitably some remain. (Usually the ones you don't like.) You'd love to take off your Manolo Blahnik's but you know you'd never get your feet back into them in this lifetime. You haven't had lipstick on for hours and you're seeing double of the guests you didn't want to invite once. The feast is over and now you have but one wish, to be in the possession of an automatic dishwasher the size of a 5-tonne truck. Instead, you're considering Maurice. He's your best friend's husband (but she passed out hours ago and hasn't been seen since her last trip to the ladies) and he's been giving you meaningful eye contact for the better part of an hour. Use him. Throw on some kind of upbeat music and dance your way into the kitchen. With any luck, he'll follow. Before he knows what's happening, you can have a dishcloth in his hand and hopefully he'll be sober enough to finish the chore.

Your beautiful dining room now resembles a scene in 'Die Hard II'. You'll probably be finding hungover guests in various rooms of your

house for the next few days. Don't despair. You've pulled it off. Pat yourself on the back. You have successfully orchestrated and delivered "The Feast for the Criminally Insane" And you thought you couldn't cook...

Preparing the Recipes

Le Potage des carotte, les pois, le maïs, le Poivron vert, l'Oignon, le Poireau et les Champignon avec un Paprik
~ or ~
Vegetable Soup

INGREDIENTS

- Butter, salted (You heard me, and if you don't keep it in your home, borrow some from your mother.) - 2 ½ tbs.
- Onion – 1 lge. Chopped finely
- Leek – 1 lge. Sliced thinly (Don't bother with the dregs of the bottom green part)
- Salt – (preferably sea salt) to taste
- Pepper – (only black freshly ground, anything else would be barbaric)
- Basil – ½ tsp. dried
- Parsley – 1 tbs. dried
- Bay leaf – 1 lge. (if you forget to remove the bay leaf before serving and somebody discovers it in their bowl and insists on taking it out with their fingers or worse it gets caught in the blinding shafts of their orthodontic hardware that this person decided to treat themselves to on their 40th birthday, don't panic. Tell them it's good luck. It works every time.)
- Paprika – lge. smidge
- Thyme – smidge

- Chili Peppers – 2 sm. crushed and chopped – optional. Jalapeno or Serrano peppers are those deadly little numbers that can be eaten but not touched. They breathe life into many recipes but if you handle them without rubber gloves and the essence gets into your eyes, look out. This is not to say that you have to protect yourself in something resembling equipment worn by the crew of Apollo 13, but it doesn't hurt. I use them all the time and have occasionally been burned. Forget water, it doesn't help. Apply butter but if you're wearing contact lenses this gets very messy. Those sissy dried chili peppers you get served in a bowl at Luigi's Ristorante are not a substitute.
- Green pepper – 1 sm. chopped finely
- Celery – 1 lge. stalk finely chopped
- Carrots – 2 med. Peeled and chopped finely
- Mushrooms – 1 ½ cups small ones, finely sliced sideways (presentation is everything) – optional
- Corn – 1 ½ cups (You could boil some fresh ears and then remove the corn, but this is a lot of hassle. Frankly, tinned corn is just as sweet, but make sure you drain it.)
- Peas – 1 cup (Again, fresh is ok if you've got all the time in the world to tear the little suckers out of their pod, but I prefer frozen.)

- Anchovies – 2 filets crushed and chopped (I know, I know, hold the pizza. Nevermind, you'll be amazed at how good they can taste. If you open up a tin just for this recipe, give the rest to the cat. You'll get cat-love for a month.) – optional
- Vegetable stock – 10-12 cups (if you can't find cubes for this, you may have to make it yourself, which is a proper pain in the you know what, see recipe below. Chicken broth is an acceptable alternative if you don't mind soup tasting like a barnyard.)
- Kiwi fruit – 1 sliced – optional

PROCEDURE

The soup can be prepared a day or 2 in advance and refrigerated then warmed slowly before serving. (When preparing the feast, you want as many of these pre-fab dishes as possible. Otherwise, you'll require the graduating class of Cordon Bleu to help you get everything ready on time.)

In a large sturdy pot, melt the butter on med. heat. Add the onion and leek and throw in some salt. Saute for a few minutes, till golden, then cover and cook 5-7 min. Add black pepper,

bay leaf, basil, parsley, thyme, crushed chili pepper. Then pour in the vegetable stock. Add carrots, green pepper, celery, bring to a boil, uncovered.

Turn heat down to simmer and add anchovies, corn and peas. Simmer for about 10 min. then add mushrooms. Simmer until all vegetables are cooked but not dead in the water.
Garnish with a slice of kiwi (or strawberry).

Vegetable Bouillon
You really wanna do this?

INGREDIENTS

- Butter (I still say salted) – 1 ½ tbs.
- Onion – 1 lge. thinly sliced
- Celery - 3 stalks finely chopped
- Carrots – 2 lge. peeled and chopped finely
- Celery salt – 1 tbs.
- Basil – 1 tbs. dried
- Bay leaves – 2 crushed
- Salt
- Ground black pepper

- Water – 3 qts. Salted (Tap water will do, unless you're cooking in an emerging nation, after all you are salting. Mineral water is fine if you've got more money than brains. Just make sure it isn't the fizzy kind.)

PROCEDURE

In a lge. heavy pot, melt the butter and sauté the onion, celery, carrots. Cover the pot and let cook for 10-12 minutes. Then add the seasoning – celery salt, basil, bay leaves, salt and pepper. Stir. Pour in the water and bring to a boil over medium heat. Then reduce heat and simmer for about 30 minutes. When it's all done, strain it through a piece of cheesecloth (preferably not one you've used to wipe down your new Jaguar with) or a sieve. (Look it up. You might even have one under your cupboard.)

Les Crêpe Française avec la Crème blanche et les Asperges
~ or ~
Asparagus in White Sauce with Pancakes

INGREDIENTS

- Water – enough to fill your steamer
- Asparagus – if they are not those really skinny ones, you should only need 2 per crepe and 3 crepes per person. Therefore, our feast being for ten people, you will need 60 spears.
- Lime juice – 1 whole lime (trust me, the bottled variety really doesn't cut it).
- Fruit sugar – 3 or 4 tbs. – optional (Whatever you do, do not substitute regular white sugar for this, we're not serving dessert.)
- Nutmeg – to taste. Just a sprinkle per crepe
- Crepes – 30 (recipe below)
- Sweet white sauce – 4 cups (recipe below)

PROCEDURE

Trim the asparagus and steam (or nuke) the spears for as long as it takes to make them tender. On a full boil steamer usually 5 – 7 minutes. Try to avoid letting the interesting ends get mushy. Take your warm crepes from wherever it is you are keeping them warm, lay flat. Add a dash of lime juice and fruit sugar then roll the 2 asparagus spears in the crepe. Lightly cover with hot white sauce.

Crepes

Just because you've watched your mother make pancakes one Saturday when you were six-years-old. Don't think this is that. We want paper thin and no lumps!

INGREDIENTS

- All purpose flour – 1 ½ cups
- Eggs – 6 lge.
- Salt – less than a tsp.
- Milk – 1 ¼ cups
- Water – 1 ¼ cups
- Butter – 6 tbs. melted

PROCEDURE

Break eggs into mixing bowl and add milk and water. Whisk. Slowly add flour and salt. Keep whisking. It should start to look like custard. Slower still, add most of the butter, drip by drip. When you're satisfied that there are no lumps, (I mean none. Nada. Zip.) melt about 1 tbs. of butter on to your professional stainless-steel crepe pan (or drag out that old wrought-iron job that your grandmother fried back bacon in and you never use, because let's face it, everything sticks to it now no matter how much grease or spray you apply and the damn thing is almost as heavy as a Volkswagen Beetle. Or any large non-stick fry pan will do.) Wipe off excessive butter. Just cover the bottom of the pan with the batter and no more. Put it back on the element (that's your stove thing) on a high heat and it will cook in seconds.

Sweet White Sauce

INGREDIENTS

- Butter – 4 tbs.
- All purpose flour – 4 tbs.
- Milk – 2 cups
- Whipping cream – 2 cups (not to be confused with that plastic, fake whipped cream you buy in a spray can like the one you've had in your fridge for an eternity just in case that gorgeous

hunk that lives next door drops by for an Irish coffee or just whipped cream…)
- Salt – pinch
- White pepper – pinch
- Sugar – 1 tbs.
- Nutmeg – pinch

PROCEDURE

Melt the butter in a heavy pot or saucepan over a low heat. Add the flour as you get whisking. After a few minutes add milk and whipping cream. Keep whisking. Gradually add salt, pepper, sugar and nutmeg. Whisk your little heart out until the sauce thickens.

Les Calmar dans la Casserole des Tomate
~ or ~
Stuffed Squid

INGREDIENTS

- Squid - 20 med.-lge. This works out to 2 per guest or if they are small make it 3 per guest. They have to be cleaned. Frankly this is not nearly as horrific as you might think. A thin skin will slide off easily. Cut off the heads but don't throw them out. Inside the tubular shaped body is a clear gel-substance reminiscent of that designer cream you've just paid a fortune for at the best cosmetic counter in town all with the hope that by rubbing it on your face it will remove the lines of aging (which any fool knows can only be alleviated by major surgery). There is also a spine that easily pops out. This looks remarkably like a piece of clear plastic that a manicurist might use to push back your cuticles. After cleaning, run the little critters under cold water. And yes, we're going to use the entire squid. That's right, curly little tentacles and all.

- Onion – 2 lge. chopped finely
- Olive oil, extra virgin (I've always wondered how that was possible) – 4 tbs.
- Salt (sea salt preferred) – lots. This is a Portuguese dish and those people love their salt not to mention seafood.
- Ground black pepper – to taste
- Red chili pepper in liquid. This too is a Portuguese thing. Absolutely delicious and can be used in lots of dishes. If you can't find it, sprinkle in some of that dried variety from Luigi's ristorante. – liquid 3 tbs. dried – 2 tbs.,
- Oregano – 1 tsp.
- Garlic – 5cloves, crushed and chopped
- Tomatoes – whole but tinned. (For our purposes, they have more flavour than ones from the vine) – 2 -28 oz. tins, slightly mashed
- Tomato paste – 10-12 oz. definitely tinned
- Rice – 2 cups Use real rice not the minute stuff. White is preferred but wild will work but not brown.
- Water – for the rice
- Butter - for the rice
- Parsley, dried – few smidges

PROCEDURE

After cleaning the squid, salt them mercilessly and let then sit.

Chop up the heads. Saute one onion in half of the olive oil until golden than add the chopped heads. Bring the water for the rice to a boil (one cup of water per one cup of rice), add a wallop of butter and some salt to the water. When it's boiling add the rice, sautéed onion and heads, liquid red chili, salt and I tsp. chopped garlic.

Cover and simmer on medium heat until the rice is cooked. (Or nuke it, if that's your way.) Let it stand five minutes or more.

While the rice is cooling, sauté the other onion in the remainder of the olive oil. In a large heavy pot, stir in the tomato paste. Add the tinned tomatoes, salt, pepper, oregano and rest of garlic. Simmer this on low heat for 30-40 minutes.

Now, comes the fun part. Stuffing the squid. (Well, what did you think we were going to do with the rice?) If the critters are large enough this isn't really a big problem. (If it so happens that you bought the small ones, give yourself more time – like maybe a day and a half.)

Fill the cavities with the cooled rice concoction and seal the end. There are many ways to do this. Sewing is fine if you're a fanatic. Stapling is not a good option because one of your guests might have a pacemaker you don't know about and the metal could set off the mechanism. (I personally only keep a stapler around to mend the hems of my skirts...) Toothpicks will do it. Toothpicks are quite amazing. I'm even thinking of dedicating a full chapter on the merits and use of toothpicks in my next book. Just remember to make your guest aware of the sharp little pieces of pointy wood when you serve.

All this can be done in advance. Add the squid into the simmering tomato sauce 15 minutes before serving. Any longer and those tired jokes about rubber bands can become all too true.

Sprinkle with parsley.

Le Sorbet du Champagne
~ or ~
Champagne Ice

INGREDIENTS

- Champagne du jour – 1 qt.
- Castor sugar – 9 oz.
- Egg whites – 4

PROCEDURE

Put 1 ½ cups of Champies into a pan then add all the sugar. Dissolve the sugar over a low heat and slowly bring to a boil. Simmer for about 10 minutes but do not stir. Remove it from the heat and let cool. It should be syrupy. After it has cooled, stir in the remainder of the champies.

Now the trick is finding the right dish to freeze it in. A 2 ½ pint freezer tray will do the trick but a friend of mine has discovered ice-cube trays. Whatever cubes she doesn't use for the sorbet, she keeps for those rainy days when her husband has the good fortune to be at work and the children are finished school for the summer and it's only the second week and they're already fighting amongst themselves physically and whining about being bored and wishing they were adopted. AND the nanny quit.

So on just such a day when she is stuck at home with the little horrors, she takes out the champagne sorbet and treats the little dears to a 'popsickle' or two until at last they fall asleep and she basks in their silent beauty that she knows she could learn to love if only they belonged to someone else.

Anyway, freeze the mixture until mushy. Then dump it into a bowl. Whisk the egg whites in something separate until they are stiff. Then fold the egg whites into the semi-frozen mixture. (Folding, for those of you who are reading this and saying – "FOLD?" – just means don't really muck up the frozen champs. Use a large spoon and lift the champs over the whites and vice-versa. Do try to get the whites evenly distributed.)

You could put the mixture into the same freezer tray but, if you really want to impress your guests, (because hopefully they are still sitting upright), use a mold. It has to be large enough to accommodate your 1 quart mixture and put a tiny bit of oil in it so that you can get the concoction out easily.

Freeze until it firms up, which is at least 2 hours. Longer if the alcohol content is abnormally high, like if the bottle you are using is some kind of champagne moonshine. (Let's face it, if that was the case, then you would have drank it long ago.)

When firm, put the mold in hot water then flip it over quickly. The sorbet should slip out. And, if you've gone to the trouble of using a mold then why not decorate your masterpiece. A few colorful berries perhaps. My friend Gizzy made a sorbet once and wanted a pretty leaf for the décor. It had to be edible so she cut a large one from her own personal marijuana plant but a few guests ate it  and ruined the rest of the dinner by insisting on wanting 'cheezies'. Nevermind, a perfect mint leaf will do nicely.

Le Lapin de Madame la Comtesse avec Biere Allemande
~ or ~
Bunny in Beer

It is almost impossible to cook les lapin incorrectly. The meat is dense and juicy and no matter what the pundits at your table say, it doesn't taste like chicken.

INGREDIENTS

- Rabbit – approx. 6 lbs. of prepared animal. This could be 2 med-lge critters or 3 small ones.
- Flour – 6 tbs. (any flour will do)
- Garlic – crushed, 1 clove
- Salt
- White pepper
- Bacon fat – ¼ cup If for some reason you don't keep your bacon fat in a tin under the sink, like the rest of us, there must be a trailer park nearby. Ask one of those folks. Otherwise, you'll have to chop

70 PREPARING THE RECIPES

up a ¼ lb. of bacon and fry it. (The bacon and the fat will both work in this recipe.)
- Butter (definitely salted – get over it!) – 2 tbs.
- Celery – 3 stalks finely chopped
- Carrots – 3 peeled and finely sliced
- Onion – 2 med.- lge. medium chopped
- Garlic – 4 cloves, crushed and chopped
- Sugar processed – 1 tbs.
- Beer – 2 bottles, preferably lager and preferably European. Anything else would just be uncivilized. Besides, domestic beer, while perfectly enjoyable on a hot afternoon or just about anytime, doesn't keep its taste when cooked. Trust me on this.

PROCEDURE

Preheat oven to 375 F. Wash the rabbit and dry it well. It always feels a little strange touching a dead, skinned carcass. You know, the little legs that used to run so fast, the little head with it's ears now cut off (Funny how we seldom feel that way about chicken. Probably because the bird has the brain the size of a pea, if at all, and most of us have never kept one as a pet.) Don't dismay, you're not dealing with "Thumper".

Cut the carcasses into medium-large pieces. Discard the heads unless you want to use them for decoration. (Just kidding.) If you really want to wimp out, you can ask your butcher to do this but if it's done too much in advance, it tends to make the meat tough.

Mix flour, ¼ of the garlic, salt and pepper in a bowl or bag and toss the bunny pieces. Shake off excess.

In a large flame-proof casserole dish with a good lid, melt the butter and bacon fat. (If you are using bacon rashers, cook the chopped up bits a little, first, before adding the butter.) Throw in the celery, carrots, onion and ½ of the garlic. Saute for 5 minutes.

Add sugar, stir. Put in the rabbit pieces and fry until browned.

Remove from heat and add the rest of the garlic as well as the beer. Put on the lid making sure that it fits tightly and put in the oven. Bake for approximately 2 hours or until rabbit is tender. (This dish can be prepared a few hours earlier and kept on a very low heat. If necessary, add a little water.)
Serve the bunny with buttered carrots, for fun. (see below)

CARROTS

Choose 2 or 3 perfect carrots per serving. Cut off the fluffy green tops and wash and reserve. Wash the carrots and steam or boil until reasonably tender. (Don't overdo them or they end up like baby food.) When serving, lay the green tops in such a way as to give the carrots the appearance of being raw. (optional)

Les Legumes verte et la Laitue Americaine
~ or ~
Salad

INGREDIENTS

- Lettuce – 1 head 'Leaf', preferably red-tipped
  1 head 'Boston'
  1 head 'Romaine'
  All washed and torn into bite-size pieces, only use the heart of the Romaine
- Red sweet pepper – 1 med. diced
- Yellow or orange sweet pepper – ½ med. diced
- Shallots or green onions or chives – 6 including the green shaft chopped
- Corn, tinned – 1 cup optional
- Grapes (seedless) – 2 cups The red variety will look more interesting on the salad but the green will do. Don't make the mistake of using purple grapes. Tasty as they may be, they have more pits then ten miles of bad road. (You don't want to know from watermelon.)
- Almonds – fistful, slivered or chopped
- Vinaigrette de la Comtesse for ½ cup

PROCEDURE

The lettuce can be torn and bagged and refrigerated in advance. (Not the previous day but hours earlier.) Make sure it has a prominent place in the fridge or you might forget about it all together. The same is true of the rest of the salad vegetables but store them separately. Toss the salad with the dressing then add the almonds.

Vinaigrette de la Comtesse

Usually the dressing would be made as we toss the salad as a form of seduction as explained in my romantic cook book – *Cooking to Bag a Mate*. But because this is a large party we can prepare it in advance and add it just before serving.

INGREDIENTS

- Dijon mustard – 2 tbs. Dijon should be a staple in any fridge. All the monopolizing, mega-business food conglomerates make some sort of Dijon. But Dijon is a place, in France, and I highly recommend one from there. It's gotta have some bite. You don't want one of those wimpy, almost, sort of, mustards and certainly not one so-yellow-it-hurts-you-eyes variety that you buy for the kids to put on their weenies. And definitely nothing with honey in it.

- Horse radish – 2 tbs. Fresh is good but completely impractical out of season. There are many good bottled ones that can knock your head off and this is of course, what we're looking for. Forget the creamed ones – yik.
- Sea salt, freshly ground to taste
- Black pepper, freshly ground to taste
- Parsley – 1 tsp. dried
- Thyme ½ tsp. dried
- Basil ½ tsp. dried
- Balsamic or red wine vinegar – 6 tbs. It never fails to impress me the conviction people have to their preference in vinegar. I can't count the number of elegant dinner parties that have been ruined when a couple of guests came to blows over vinegar. But one thing they all agree on is that vinegar must be expensive. The other stuff they sell in huge plastic jugs should only be used for washing floors. (For more information please read Sybil Drysdale's captivating text – *Culinary Cleansers*.)

- Olive oil, extra virgin – ¼ cup
- Lemon – juice of ½ fresh lemon

PROCEDURE

Whisk together the mustard, salt, pepper, parsley, thyme, basil and vinegar. Then slowly add the oil and lemon juice and keep whisking. This dressing will keep in the fridge for weeks. Shake it before application.

L'enremets Rustique avec les Peche dans le Jaques Daniels
~ or ~
Trifle with Jack

INGREDIENTS

- Milk – 1 pt. This is definitely not the time to wimp out and use 2% or worse, skim. You need whole milk. If you still have some sitting in the back of your fridge from the last time your friends with the children-from-hell visited (you know the little darlings that played trampoline on your new Laura Ashley duvet cover while wearing their $200.00-plus running shoes that are so high-tech they should require a license just to do them up. And… after playing hide n' seek in your clothes closet where they discovered your private lingerie collection worth thousands, not to mention a few assorted "toys" and then came back into the living room wearing much of it on their heads, when their parents, the people you used to go clubbing with but you can hardly recognize because of the perpetual tortured looks on their faces and a new-found disregard for cosmetics, chided the little pumpkins and after they all finally

left, it took three days to find the dog who was pitiably cowering in the basement) I suggest you read the expiry date on the carton of milk or just buy some fresh.
- Custard powder – 3 tbs. You're probably going to have to buy this, but it does come in tins and lasts forever. My tin of custard powder goes back to my grandmother. It is one of those curious culinary staples that you use once in a blue moon but ceremoniously hand it down with the other family heirlooms.
- Sugar – 2 tbs. white, granulated
- Coarse bread – ½ loaf, cut into tablespoon-size pieces with crusts off. This is best if it is day old or dense like Tuscany bread.
- Marmalade – 3 tbs. Other thick sweet jams or preserves will do but the orange of marmalade works well with bourbon.
- Strawberries – 6-8 large sliced
- Tangerine – 1 peeled and sectioned
- Peaches – one 19 oz. tin
- Sherry dry – 5 tbs.
- Brandy or Bourbon – ¼ cup or to taste. I find that as I prepare a trifle and the bread absorbs the alcohol, I tend to keep adding more. Beware of this. The few remaining guests that are still managing a sensible conversation could be reduced to snorting through lewd, bawdy jokes that are made up mostly of four-letter

words and involve Rabbis and priests or little boys named Johnny and which no longer make you laugh since you already know the punch lines.

- ∾ Whipping cream – ¼ pt. (see Whipping cream note under Sweet white sauce).

PROCEDURE

In a mixing bowl, blend 6 tbs. of the milk with the custard powder and sugar. Bring the rest of the milk to a boil in a saucepan. Pour boiling milk over the powder mixture and stir well. Put the milk and powder mixture back in the saucepan and bring it all back to a boil. Keep stirring until it thickens. Take it off the burner to cool. (Sometimes a skin forms. You can take it off if it grosses you out but all I usually do is stir it back in, unless it has become as thick as the sole of a Berkenstock.)

Spread the marmalade over the bread and reserve half. Place half in the bottom and up the sides of the serving bowl. Cover with sliced strawberries and sections of tangerines. (Keep a few of each for decorating the top.)

Mix 4 tbs. of the syrup from the peaches with the alcohol.

Drizzle half of this liquid over the bread and fruit. Arrange the rest of the marmalade bread as another layer and cover with peaches. (Again, reserve a few for decoration.) Drizzle the rest of the liquid over top.

Go back to the mixture cooling in the saucepan and beat it. When it becomes like a custard, pour it over the fruit and put in the fridge for at least one hour.

Whip the cream until it is stiff. Cover the top of your dessert and decorate. I've found that people are pretty much over "Happy Face". How about an aerial view of the Great Wall of China, or not. You'll think of something.

Acknowledgements

So many people to thank. First to my close friend and confidante, Madame le Pot de Chambre who once said, "You should write a book!" I am eternally grateful.

Mr. and Mrs. Kent-Graves-Southby for their inspiring lecture series – "What's to be done with leeks". You made my summer.

La Comtesse d'Evinrude's gardener's wife, Maria, for the thoughtful advice on how to legally dispose of the remains of a bovine carcass. The mottled bar stool covers have been an endless source of conversation at my dinner parties.

To my dentist, Doctor Jean la Foret who told me with a straight face that eating green vegetables can be as good for the teeth as flossing, and then presenting me with a bill for his consultation.

Thanks also to my tailor, Monsieur Henri, who magically altered my size 6 wardrobe to accommodate my burgeoning size10 form while only making me look size 8.

To my hairdresser, Monsieur Wayne of Wawa, what can I say? With your great dexterity, patience, dare I say – talent, and very few snits, you managed to coiffe my fading tresses enough to camouflage the second and third chins that have recently developed. And who recommended an excellent plastic surgeon, to whom *he* is eternally grateful.

Special thanks to my publisher, without whom I couldn't have been published.

Thanks for all those fabulous feasts, real or imagined, that I have been served by gracious friends and relevant restauranteurs.

And finally, Monsieur Jacques Daniels for... well... just the inspiration.

Bibliography

A Cloistered Nun's Guide to Religious Sorbet
By Sister Mary-Margaret of the Sisters of Perpetual Sorrow

A Little Lamb
By Mary

Chili Peppers, Then and Now
By Poncho Villa

Eating on a Full Stomach
By O. Welles

Enjoying Your Friends and Acquaintances
By Jeffrey Dalmer

How to Prepare your Enemy for Dinner
By Man Friday

Hunting for Game, Stalking it, Killing it, Skinning it and Preparing it
By M. Perkins

Keeping your Hare
By E. Fudd

Lettuce, the Whole Picture
By J. Childe

Looking for Game in all the Wrong Places
By Quinn the Inuit

Rabbits I Have Known and Loved
By MacDonald, the Elder

Salad, Salad, Salad
By M. Ghandi

Secrets of the Soup Kitchen
By Major MacKenzie

Sorbet and You
By M. Quant

Take My Squid, Please...
By H. Youngman

The Agony and Ecstasy of Chili Pepper
By Juan Cuervera

The Dangers of Watermelon Seeds and Other Precarious Dining Adventures
By A. Warhol

The Healing Properties of Garlic OR How to Lose Friends and Distance People
By I. Amin

Torture and Tortellini
By the Marquis de Sade

Trifle in Our Times
By R. M. Nixon

Watermelon as a Last Choice
By Lady Astor

What? Me, Curry?
By A. E. Neumann

What to do with Stale Bread and Grape Juice
By anonymous from the Vatican

A Note From the Publisher

Madame la Comtesse le Visage du Bouvier (not her real name) prefers to be known as Wallis Merrick-Lincoln (also not her real name). She came into her great wealth the old-fashioned way, she married it... And not just once.

Madame is the self-acclaimed author of *Cellphones for Schizophrenics* a crazy look at crazy people. *Hairplugs and Ferraris* the mid-life crisis – real or imagined – oh, it's real all right and *Dentists on Harleys* what you didn't know about Sheldon.

Although various languages have been referenced in this manuscript, any misspellings are entirely intentional.

The Reviews

"Don't try this at home! No really!"
raves the Auto Mechanics and Gourmet Cooking magazine.

"You must be joking or is that choking"
quips The Trailer Park Restaurant Guide.

"What the heck, go ahead and try it, I dare you"
penned by The S&M Alternative Lifestyle newspaper.

"Madame who?"
queries The consular general of the government of France.

"Is this the Madame at the Pink Pearl Massage Parlour?"
- Anonymous

About the Author

Madame La Comtesse le Visage du Bouvier is also known as Diane Stead.

Diane Stead has written 3 novels, all thrillers – *Video Pals*, *The Monument Murders*, *The Delos Murders*. Also she has written several episodes of various television programs from soap operas to hour-long crime dramas.

She is extensively travelled and lives with her husband in Toronto.

Special thanks to AME for all the illustrations; James Sweetland for the front and back cover artwork; Gary Van Netten for the cover photographs and Curtis Gaudon for assembling all of the above.

www.ingramcontent.com/pod-product-compliance
Lightning Source LLC
Chambersburg PA
CBHW021019090426
42738CB00007B/826